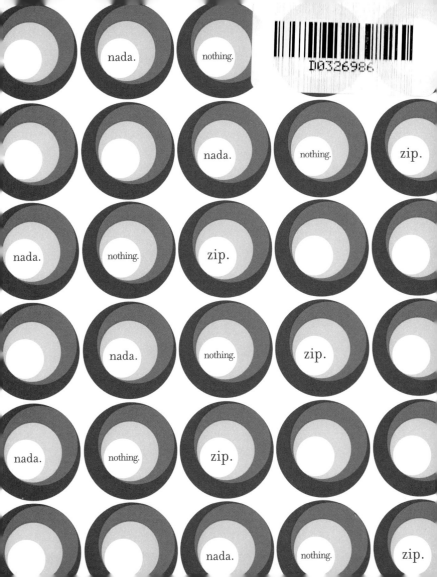

Simon & Schuster
Rockefeller Center
1230 Avenue of the Americas
New York, NY 10020

Copyright © 2003 by Karen Salmansohn
Book packaged by Karen Salmansohn/Glee Industries

SIMON & SCHUSTER and colophon are registered trademarks
of Simon & Schuster, Inc.

For information regarding special discounts for bulk purchases,
please contact Simon & Schuster Special Sales at 1-800-456-6798
or business@simonandschuster.com

Manufactured in the United States of America
3 5 7 9 10 8 6 4 2

Library of Congress Cataloging-in-Publication Data
Salmansohn, Karen.
How to change your entire life by doing absolutely nothing : 10 do-nothing
relaxation exercises to calm you down quickly so you can speed
forward faster/Karen Salmansohn.
p.   cm.
1. Change (Psychology) 2. Self-actualization (Psychology) I. Title.
BF637.C4.S24   2003   158.1—dc21   2002033301

ISBN 0-7432-4472-9

HOW TO CHANGE YOUR ENTIRE LIFE BY DOING ABSOLUTELY NOTHING

[
10 DO-NOTHING RELAXATION EXERCISES
TO CALM YOU DOWN QUICKLY
SO YOU CAN SPEED FORWARD FASTER
]

WRITTEN AND ILLUSTRATED BY

KAREN SALMANSOHN

Simon & Schuster

New York   London   Toronto   Sydney   Singapore

WARNING #1:

Before you start any exercise program, please consult your doctor—oh, to hell with that!

This is the world's first exercise program where you won't have to worry about breaking a sweat—or a nail. In fact you'll barely be moving your tush or a neuron!

Because, frankly, your neurons have been behaving like morons, speedily dashing around, confusing movement with forward motion.

This exercise program will train your pesky neurons to sit still and DO NOTHING for a change so that you can move forward faster and get some life change.

WARNING #2:

Before you read any further, you must ask yourself are you ready to change your entire life? Because, if you regularly follow these do-nothing relaxation exercises, you will experience a surge of energy, power, clarity, and speed . . . like you've never experienced before.

Plus, you will be the beneficiary of the #1 favorite exercise result: wait loss!

Wait loss in getting the career you want, love you want, whatever the heck you want!

Yes, you are about to discover a cheery, paradoxical life principle:

Sometimes the shortest distance between two points is DOING ABSOLUTELY NOTHING.

WARNING #3:

Nike is wrong. Just do nothing.

Confession time . . .

One night I was busy doing my bills and folding my laundry while watching a TV special about transsexuals, and I found one thought—and one thought only—went racing through my mind:

Where do these people find the time to go for such extensive sex-change operations? I barely had time to pay my bills and get new vacuum cleaner bags let alone get new sexual organs. It seemed I always had a list of 20 things to do—with only time to do 10—and somehow I always managed to squoosh in 30.

My life was starting to remind me of Ray Bradbury's book *Fahrenheit 451*, in which Ray describes a society where you must drive over 55 mph, so you cannot see the world around you clearly. In this blurry, fast-paced world, porches have been banned, so you don't have a place to sit and feel what you may sit and feel. And books have been burned, so you cannot be inspired to think deeply. All too often in my busy whirlwind world I was finding that I barely had time to sit/feel/think deeply.

My motto had become:

"So much to do, so little time to do it all but, thankfully, plenty of time to complain about having no time to do it all."

(I sometimes even wondered whether I'd have anything to talk about if I didn't complain!)

As we all know, the first step to curing a drinking problem is to accept you have a drinking problem. Same goes for a thinking problem, which I was starting to suspect that I might have.

It seemed that every day I was reaching for the first handy negative, stressful thought I had within reach. Sometimes even first thing in the morning. The alarm would go off, and so would my internal alarms. I'd wake up thinking: "Okay, I'll just think this one negative thought about my life—then stop." Next thing I knew, before I'd even showered, I was pouring nonstop toxic thoughts into my brain: "Oh, how my relationship sucks! My life sucks! The world sucks! Distant galaxies suck!"

Before I knew it,
I'd completely
conjugated the
verb . . .

"to suck."

(Then it hit me: Uh-oh, I had a heavy-duty
thinking problem—and I needed help!)

I needed to
calm down—
quickly—

ASAP!

Of course I recognized that "calming down quickly ASAP" sounded a wee bit contradictory. I also knew I didn't have gobs of time to waste calming down in a calm fashion. I am a busy person. In fact, I am the person who invented "multitasking." Yup, that was me. (If only I'd thrown a little ™ on my multitasking invention, I'd be a very rich woman today.)

So what does the person who invented multitasking do to relax?

ANSWER:

Multitask

DO-NOTHING
RELAXATION
EXERCISES

into one's day.

For example:

Do-nothing exercise #1:

Wake Up and Smell the Coffee

fig. 1   fig. 2   fig.3

On the very morning I realized I had a thinking problem, I was ready to start on my toxic thinking spree when I decided to stop and drink coffee instead—but really DO NOTHING but drink my coffee. For the next 10 minutes I forced myself not to think or talk about my problems. I just stopped and smelled the coffee. (Whiffed that wafting aroma.) I saw the coffee. (Stared at the pretty milk swirls.) Tasted the coffee. (Savored every good to bitter to best nuance.) I became the coffee. (Went from coffee bean to coffee being.) And if/when I found my anxious morning mind drifting to upsetting work or love problems, I redirected it back to my coffee's aroma, and stopped my mind from a-roaming to negative thoughts.

I did this for 10 minutes.

Straight.

(Nada a negative
neuron in sight.)

One hour later, I finally "cracked the code" on a writing project I'd been tortured by for the last month. Shazam: the writing came torrenting out of my fingers. It was bizarre. I knew it wasn't just the caffeine that was to be credited. In fact I can even now confidently say that I feel caffeine gets more credit than it deserves when it comes to inspiration—and that any prior "coffee breaks" that led to "coffee breakthroughs" occurred because I was unwittingly doing a DO-NOTHING EXERCISE.

That's when I had an epiphany: If multitasking this one 10-minute DO-NOTHING COFFEE EXERCISE into my day worked so well, then, damn, I should try to multitask in other DO-NOTHING EXERCISES. So, I created these . . .

Do-Nothing Exercise #2: Shower Power

Every shower I now take, I now multitask in washing away my stress and anxieties, by DOING NOTHING but concentrating on the concentration of water spritzing down upon me. I do not think or worry about how hot or cold my love or career life is—only about the water's temperature, flow, feel, volume. I become aware of every element of this element—for at least 5 minutes.

fig.1   fig.2   fig.3

Do-Nothing
Exercise #3:
Mellow
Yellow

On my way to or from meeting with an exasperating or annoying or "challenging" person, I now search for the color yellow. Whenever I find my brain drifting to something truly annoying and goofball-like about this person that makes me want to yell, I DO NOTHING but seek yellow. Yes, instead of seeing red I see yellow—for at least 5 minutes.

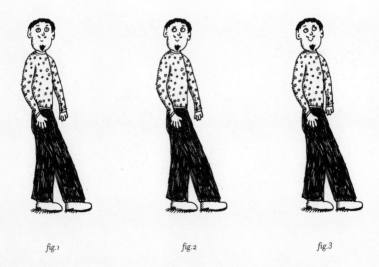

fig.1   *fig.2*   *fig.3*

Do-Nothing Exercise #4:
Like Attracts Like, Glee Attracts Glee

Anytime within a day that I find myself thinking stressful, negative thoughts, I decide to flood my mind with positive words instead. For instance, if I want to be more calm, I DO NOTHING but think up words that mean "calm": peaceful, tranquil, serene, mellow, balanced, harmonious, shhhhhhhhhh— for at least 5 blissful, composed, easygoing minutes. Or if I'm sad about something, I think up words that make me gleeful, mirthful, cheery, happy, jaunty, lighthearted, peppy, upbeat, fulfilled—and fill my brain with these.

fig.1   *fig.2*   *fig.3*

Do-Nothing Exercise #5:
Hear the Beat to Beat the Blues

If during a day I get a phone call that's bad news, I put on a good CD—and DO NOTHING but hear the beat in the music until it beats my blues away. I sit and listen to the drums and only the drums, feel the beat pulse through my body, and match my breathing with the beat—for at least 5 minutes.

fig.1   *fig.2*   *fig.3*

After I began regularly multitasking all of this DO-NOTHINGNESS into my day, I felt as if I'd discovered a sneaky secret, because I was making decisions faster, solving problems more swiftly, speeding through my workload—plus, I was now able to use that impressive word . . .

dichotomy

(I love that word!)

"Yes, it's such a dichotomy," I began telling my friends, "how all this slowing down has speeded me up. It's **kinda weird**, huh?"

But I'm a practical person, so I wanted to figure out a nonweird explanation for why these DO-NOTHING EXERCISES work.

Thankfully,
I came up with this
practical explanation
right here:

DO-NOTHING
EXERCISES
=
ENERGY
MANAGEMENT

It's like this.
All your thoughts have
energy. Meaning:

Scattered/negative/
out-of-control thoughts =
scattered/negative/
out-of-control energy.

Controlled/managed/
channeled thoughts =
controlled/managed/
channeled energy.

Symptoms of scattered/negative/ out-of-control thoughts:

1. You try to gain control of the unknown by guessing what will happen next.

2. You try to wrestle old demons to the ground, obsessing about your past.

3. You try to busy your mind with work or personal problems or any negative thought and don't allow positive, gleeful thoughts in.

Yup. I was guilty of scattered / negative / out-of-control thinking.

No wonder when I stopped and rechanneled my thinking—with DO-NOTHING EXERCISES—I had so much more energy to think and see more clearly.

Basically, DO-NOTHING EXERCISES were saving me from wasting precious brain energy that could be better used to propel my consciousness to superconsciousness.

And as I later learned, DO-NOTHING EXERCISES not only worked for logical reasons but biological ones, too.

I've since read how biologists have found—in study after study—that stopping to DO NOTHING slows down brain waves, decreases blood pressure, increases blood circulation, increases overall energy levels, reduces stress, and strengthens the immune system.

Well, my own one-human DO-NOTHING study also proved all the biologists' research to be true, because I found that after I stopped scattering my energy on worry, fear, doubt, and anxiety and began redirecting my brain to stay present in the moment, I started to experience major surges of energy, speed, clarity—and even good fortune.

ALL OF THIS REMINDED ME OF THAT FAMOUS
SERENITY PRAYER:

Please, God, give me the serenity
to accept the things I cannot
change, the courage to change the
things I can, and the wisdom to
know the difference.... And let
my dry cleaning be ready on
Tuesday.

(OR THE PRAYER THAT GOES SOMETHING LIKE THAT.)

(ANYWAY.
MY POINT . . .)

After multitasking

into my day, I found
I was much better
able to sense the
senselessness and
sensefulness of what I
could and could not
change . . . and sense
how to change what
needed changing.

Thankfully,
I was able to
sense yet another
logical explanation
for this as well:

THE PARETER PRINCIPLE.

(Read on . . .)

THE PARETER PRINCIPLE explains how successful results come from 20 percent of your actions. When you calm down your mind you develop 20/20 vision to see which actions are your 20 percent priority actions. Then you can redirect the saved 80 percent of your time and energy into accomplishing this 20 percent in a faster, smarter way.

Cool, huh?

Buddhists have a single word for this process of DO-NOTHING energy management:

MINDFULNESS.

Though in many ways mindfulness is more like mind-un-full-ness, because this process is about emptying your mind of its ceaseless chattering so you can better see and understand the world around you.

Yes, it seems millions of
Buddhists and I all agree:
"Damn, it's ironic how when you
stop and do nothing you can move
more quickly forward—and be
wiser at determining what life
switches to switch, what levers to
lever, what lovers to leave."

DO-NOTHING EXERCISES
create something I call
"hocus focused
energy magic."
When I stopped
scattering my
thoughts on worry,
fear, and angst, I
discovered I could
focus more strongly on
where to find my
misplaced miracle.

And I've since come to believe that a big reason why hindsight comes with 20/20 vision is because of hocus focused energy magic. When everything done is done, you're no longer distracted by negative, fearful emotions.

Removing this emotional static is like getting cable hookup. Not only is your picture of the situation clearer, you have more viewing options and are better able to view a problem from more perspectives. And the more perspectives you have, the more of a shot you have at finding the right path to getting what you want.

I believe that when William Blake wrote "If the doors of perception were cleansed everything would appear to man as it is: infinite," what he was *really* trying to say is "There are always infinite possibilities to solving problems and getting what you want, and stopping your brain from scattering its energy by practicing DO-NOTHING EXERCISES is like applying Windex to your window on the world."

(T<small>HOUGH</small>, <small>GRANTED</small>,
<small>THIS</small> B<small>LAKE DUDE</small>'<small>S</small>
<small>QUOTE IS A BIT MORE</small>
<small>POETIC THAN MY OWN</small>.)

And I believe that when Peter Ouspenky wrote "The subconscious mind functions at as much as 30,000 times the speed of your conscious mind," what he was *really* trying to say is "If you can tap into your subconscious, you have 30,000 times the advantage, seeing things 30,000 times faster and clearer than ordinary folks."

(Though I'm
sort of kidding . . .
and sort of not.)

Basically, if you can clear away the clutter of your often imaginary worries and fears and instead hear your subconscious, then you definitely have quite a huge lead in the Awareness of Reality Department.

When I think about "the subconscious,"
my conscious mind thinks about
old Jung who wrote:

"When a situation is not made conscious,
it appears outside as fate."

These "fates" can be anything from losing
your house keys to breaking a leg . . . and are
attempts by your subconscious to help you
face up to your true inner needs.

Losing house keys =
needing to get out of your
house to get more stuff done.

Breaking your leg =
needing to stay home
more and do less.

Your subconscious knows
lots about you. It has the inside
scoop on what needs to
be changed—and how—
and is working . . .

24/7

to pass on this helpful info to you.

It even works all night, while you are asleep. Yes, according to Jung, your dreams are your sub-conscious mind's attempt to (YO!) get your attention.

Considering all the subconscious does, it should be granted "above" rather than "sub" conscious status, because it often winds up making more life decisions than the conscious. It's actually your subconscious that's in charge of how many sick days you get, how messy your apartment is, even how messy your love life is. And your subconscious is also responsible for why your diary often looks like Madlibs:

Dear Diary:

I'm.......(miffed, resentful, glum) that my.......(new paramour, old paramour, future paramour) doesn't.......(listen to me more, respect me more, adore me more). It reminds me of what happened.......(last week, last month, last year, next week, next month, next year). I swear to....... (GOD, BUDDHA, MY MANICURIST). I won't let this happen again!

Your subconscious is secretly (and craftily)
hoping that all your repeated

"bad fates"

will eventually awake you to seek change.
It's hoping to get you sick and tired of how
things are going, and often it literally and
physically makes you "sick and tired."

I've read how
Taoists call the
state of being
sick and tired
a *kriya*
. . . which means
something like
having a spiritual
tantrum that leads
to an awakening.

ME, PERSONALLY, I'VE CALLED IT:

"the breakup that
led to the breakdown
that led to the
breakthrough."

I've found it's usually after a good, long *kriya* that I'm finally willing to change—and thereby able to fill in those diary blanks with cheerier words.

The problem is that all too often I put off my *kriya*—like putting off a trip to the dentist—until the pain is unbearable.

Do-NOTHING EXERCISES are like getting an advanced X-ray view of the subconscious, and can thereby save you major emotional pain to come— if you just look at those damn X rays— look at your damn subconscious thoughts.

And DO-NOTHING exercises also help you to see what I call the "SUB-SUB-CONSCIOUS" —or what everyone else calls "INTUITION"!

BECAUSE OF THE

NOW.

HOW?

DO-NOTHING EXERCISES place you fully in the NOW where you have no anxiety about "fear of pain from your future" or "fear of pain from your past" because you don't give a darn about the past or future . . . only about the NOW.

Yes, when you are DOING NOTHING and THINKING NOTHING but NOW thoughts you are better able to view your fears without fear, the same way you are able to more clearly see your life in "hindsight"—because in the now there is no fear.

Chogyam Trungpa, author of *Shambala: The Sacred Path of the Warrior*, said it well when he said:

"True fearlessness is not the reduction of fear; but going beyond fear. Unfortunately in the English language we don't have one word that means that. Fearlessness is the closest term, but by fear-less we don't mean 'LESS FEAR,' but 'BEYOND FEAR.'"

And we are all in this "beyond-fear place" whenever we are in a wildly sudden, scary place—like a car crash—when we don't have time to obsess about our fears. We must only be in the now—and NOW—doing what needs to be done NOW to survive, even if this means doing what's usually never done—like lifting an 800-pound car off one's leg . . .

NOW!

NOW!

NOW!

We wind up being able to lift that car because we are channeling all of our hither-to-now, non-now past/future, fearful, stressful, scattered energies toward this one GET THIS CAR OFF ME NOW goal.

Yes.

(The power of now
has lots of power.)

And not only does being in the now come in handy in scary situations like car crashes but also in scary situations like job interviews, first dates, last dates, etc., because this place of now is a place of power that gives you that aforementioned hocus focused energy magic.

Soon after realizing all of this, I also realized—being the multitasker inventor that I am—that I needed to find a way to multitask even more NOTHINGNESS into my life.

So I did . . .

and now do.

(FOR EXAMPLE . . .)

I now DO NOTHING when I need to go to work. I now DO NOTHING when I need to clean up. I now DO NOTHING when I need to get something to eat. I now DO NOTHING when I need to go to the gym. I now DO NOTHING when I need to get ready for bed.

FOR EXAMPLE:

DO-NOTHING EXERCISE #6: LISTEN TO SOUNDS FOR A SOUNDER MIND

On my way to meet someone, I now DO NOTHING but revel in whatever background sounds are on the street, bus, subway—whatever my transportation mode du jour—and I've found multitasking in listening to background sounds gives me a sounder mind and heart.

fig.1

fig.2

fig.3

Do-Nothing Exercise #7: Smells like Relaxation

I now pick cleaning products for their scents, rather than because they save me cents. And instead of focusing on the drudgery of cleaning, I now DO NOTHING but appreciate the new, fresher scent in the air around me. And whenever I'm doing my (ugh) laundry . . . I now DO NOTHING but relish the aroma of my loved one's shirt . . . notice both its sweetness and sweatiness.

fig.1

fig.2

fig.3

Do-Nothing
Exercise #8:
Thought for Food

Whenever/whatever I'm eating—lunch, dinner, snack, airplane food—I now DO NOTHING but concentrate on every gustory-laden bite—for at least 5 minutes. I stop wolfing, gulping, scarfing and start focusing on all those flavor nuances: savory, sweet, bitter, citrusy, chocolatey. (In fact, lately I've even started to do special "Do-Nothing Chocolate Exercises" where I just focus on the chocolate, chocolate, chocolate—you know, all for the sake of my balanced mental health, of course!)

fig. 1   fig. 2   fig. 3

DO-NOTHING EXERCISE #9: STRONG MIND, STRONG BODY

Now when I work out my body I multitask working out my mind—building up strong thought muscles. I no longer work out willy-nilly, but instead focus my mind to truly think about each individual muscle group. Whenever I find my mind wandering to a problem, fear, worry, I force my mind to envision every muscle strand getting stronger and stronger— for at least 5 minutes.

fig.1   fig.2   fig.3

Do-Nothing Exercise #10:
Wake Up Your Senses Before Bedtime

Now whenever I go to sleep, I go to sleep rapt with rapture—not wrapped in flannel! Before I climb into bed, I make sure that my paramour and I have stripped completely down to nothing so we can DO-NOTHING. (NOTE: Well, at least we DO NOTHING for 5 minutes. After that, not to worry, a lot of NON-NOTHING stuff can/will/should happen.)

Anyway, for 5 minutes we DO NOTHING but luxuriate in the feel of each other's skin. (And if no paramour is available, I make sure I have fresh-smelling, silky sheets and I DO NOTHING, but feel their silkiness against my skin—for 5 minutes.)

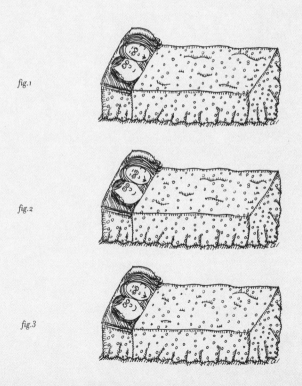

fig.1

fig.2

fig.3

Yes, I must confess, I now not only start my day DOING NOTHING. I end my day DOING NOTHING . . . and in between I multitask in as much DO-NOTHINGNESS as possible—even more do-nothingness than I ever thought possible! And ever since I started this DO-NOTHING EXERCISE PROGRAM, I've discovered that I have more power, energy, clarity, speed than I ever thought possible.

So . . . what more can I say about how beneficial DOING NOTHING is to helping someone to change his entire life?

ABSOLUTELY
NOTHING.

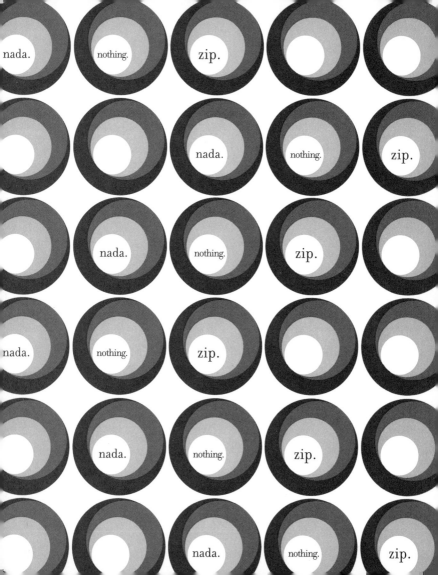